"...and the two shall become one"

For Better or... FOR WORSE

S.J. Boykin

Copyright © 2002 by S.J. Boykin
For Better or...For Worse

All rights reserved. No part of this publication may be reproduced, stored in a retrieval system, or transmitted, in any form or by any means, electronic, mechanical, photocopying, recording, or otherwise, without the written prior permission of the author.

Unless otherwise indicated, all scripture in this book is from the New King James translation.

ISBN – 978-1-387-71703-3

Book Cover Design by Inspired Writer's Ink
Published by Golden by Design – gbdp.leighbivens.org

Miami, Florida

iii

Acknowledgements

I would like to take this opportunity to thank *God*, our *Father*, *Jesus our Savior* and *His Holy Spirit our Teacher* whom I acknowledge in all I do so that He can direct my path.

I express my love to my husband *Apostle Benjamin J. Boykin*, who has shown me through the good and the challenging that it does make a difference when we "count it all joy". I love you and pray that our marriage continues to be as exciting as it was the first day we laid eyes on each other.

To my six children, *Eric, Andrea, Quadir, Zakiyyah, Erica,* and *Sherrelle* along with my daughter-in-law, *Talia* and son's-in-law *Brian* and *Demetrius*, and all my grandchildren, you have given me years of memories, of testing God's Word and the importance of love and loyalty It was all worth it. You have shown me in my older years that whatever I put my mind to I can accomplish it. I love you and pray your marriages are just as important to you as you have seen in your dad and me.

I also thank all those that have prayed and labored with me to make this possible.

To my *True Fellowship Worship Center Family*, you are my heartbeat and I love you so very much.

Special thanks to you my secret inspiration, *Minister Leigh Bivens.*

This information and research has come from various authors, booklets and publications. I have used different versions of the Bible to get scripture clarification. I appreciated the many forms of information that was distributed, and brief quotes and excerpts have been taken from many of these resources.

vi

Dedication

I dedicate this book to the memory of my Mother, **Sr. Pastor Myrtis Armbrister,** who prayed for her 5 children that God would establish us in a good marriage. She was a woman of prayer.

viii

Table of Contents

Introduction...11

Chapter 1: What Is Marriage?...13

Chapter 2: Putting God First in All You Do!................15

Chapter 3: Who Told You God Joined You Together?...........19

Chapter 4: What Is Intimacy?...25

Chapter 5: Doing the Right Thing, Even If It Means Not Winning! …..29

Chapter 6: Handle Your Finances.................................35

Chapter 7: How Can Two Walk Together If They Don't Agree?.............41

Chapter 8: Partners for Life...45

About the Author..49

Endnotes..51

x

Introduction

Marriage, from the beginning, has always been a mysterious form of union. Throughout history marriage has been thought of as a ritual, agreement, contract, policy, conveyance and even business. The idea that God established in the joining of two people has been distorted and abused for centuries, and now it is time for change.

In light of what society has done to the sacred union of marriage we still must remember that Marriage is a covenant established between two consenting parties, one male and the other female, ordained and witnessed by God the Father, God the Son (Jesus) and God the Holy Spirit. Ask yourself, "Who can spiritually and naturally take one person, cause a deep sleep to rest upon them, take out one rib and form another life, then states a covenant promise over their lives that from that day forth they shall become bone of each other's bones and flesh of each other's flesh?" This was so precious and meaningful to the man that he declares his undying dedication to the woman of his life that he will never forsake her but grow closer and stronger with her (Genesis 2:21-25). God is that Creator of this never-ending covenant.

It is time for us to begin to examine ourselves and the purpose we have in mind when we decide that our lives will be filled with someone who will begin to share in things we are about. Yet, I strongly feel that God is bringing marriages to the forefront because He is revealing the time we are coming in and that is the dispensation of preparing ourselves as Brides to meet our Bride Groom:

Joel 2:16, Gather the people, sanctify the congregation, assemble the elders, gather the children, and those that suck the breasts: let the bridegroom go forth of his chamber, and the bride out of her closet.

Therefore, marriage is being targeted and challenged so widely and in so many ways.

As we go forth in this brief but fulfilling manual I pray that His Holy Spirit bless, instruct, inform, strengthen, draw closer, give insight and empower every lesson that is to be engraved on our hearts.

Prayerfully the sanctity of marriage will be brought back to the original format and keep in the secrets of our hearts, teaching us to love, honor and respect those that God has joined together.

A Marriage Prayer

Lord as we go forward in this book we pray that you will speak to our hearts and give us the knowledge we need to receive the soul mate you are giving us. Thank you, Lord, for your direction in everything we do. Amen.

Chapter 1

What Is Marriage?

*W*ebster's dictionary describes marriage as the mutual relation between husband and wife; the institution in which a man and a woman are joined in a special social and legal relationship for the purpose of making a home and raising a family; an intimate or close union. This is a good description; however, it is only a mere formality of what marriage begins with.

What Is Marriage? It is a *"COVENANT"* that requires two individuals to become bound to each other to fulfill certain conditions and promises.

During biblical times, in making covenants, God was considered as a witness in the vow and approved the covenant with some form of seal. In marriage, this seal is honored with rings.

The marriage contract is called *"the covenant of God"* (**Proverbs 2:17**). Here, Solomon conveys to his son to not forsake Wisdom as a woman should not forsake her husband from the days of her youth or beginning. He compares it to the "not committing adultery" portion of the Ten Commandments God established in Exodus 20:14, and because it clearly states that God is a witness in the covenant, it assures me that marriage is between a man and a woman. God ordained marriage in the example of Adam and Eve and was firmly the only witness they had. God is not going to be in anything that is not righteous in His eyes. Marriage was predestined as a righteous ceremony

13

because it is in right standing with God when done under the ordinances of God.

Marriage is one of the deepest and most spiritual unions of a man and a woman, ordained by God (**Genesis 2:24**). The Hebrew and Greek meaning for marriage is *"to take"*, that is a wife; *"to magnify"* or *"to lift up"* a woman, *"to dwell together"*. These words take on such a prolific and exhilarating message of love. For when a man takes a woman to be his lawful wife he therefore goes on a journey that will never cease from having many different types of emotions, feelings, benefits and promises as never before. What is being established in this union is another society that is to be governed by the Husband in the way that Christ governs the Church. This is with love and not fear, patience and not anxiety, peace and not confusion. The idea of marriage is to be able to dwell together in agreement and esteem each other higher than yourselves, placing no strongholds on each other's dreams and visions as long as they bring edification and enrichment to the community which is your generation. Let us begin to change our way of thinking and start conforming to what God designed for our good.

A Marriage Prayer

Lord we know that you have ordained and consecrated the sanctity of marriage. For those of us that are married, teach us to be good examples to those who desire marriage. Help us to understand your will for our union. Amen.

Chapter 2

Putting God First in All You Do

Trust in the Lord with all thine heart; and lean not unto thine own understanding. In all thy ways acknowledge him, and he shall direct thy paths (Proverbs 3:5-6).

This is one of my favorite scriptures of instruction. I found that in this particular passage it releases me from trying to work things out on my own. When I am in obedience to God He gives me the direction and ability to move forward into my destiny. But, the one thing we lack is faithfulness.

In this segment, my goal is to convince or persuade each couple that the only way you can succeed in anything you do is to first question God about what you want Him to do first in your plans. Ask Him if this is His plan or a self-plan.

Scripture speaks of it and it's the one thing that is very difficult to gain and very easy to lose - "**TRUST**." When trust is out of any relationship it ceases from being bi-lateral and moves to unilateral. Decisions are now made without considering the other person involved and situations began to arise that will not go away until they have destroyed everyone and everything it encounters. That's why it is important to first trust God and His decisions, His plans, His directions, His purpose, etc... Knowing this, when we come together as one and trust God in all things we will not question or find fault in each other because the decisions we make are made through the Holy Spirit and His divine plan for us.

Let's look at the word faithful. This is a word of challenge. To be faithful is to be committed. According to [2]Webster - *"faithful"* means to maintain allegiance, showing constant loyalty, having a strong sense of duty or responsibility. In every portion of our lives we have been committed or dedicated to someone or something with a devoted pledge to preserve and keep the fervent love in our hearts for whatever it may be until it is no longer with us. This could have been our parents, children, jobs, and even our possessions. God is calling for us to rearrange our lives and begin to look at Him as the main pipeline we need to divert our attention to and give our loyalty to (Deuteronomy 5:7-9).

As we begin to place our lives in the order that God intended and start our relationship of trust in the Father then we will find that this builds our natural relationships into a whole new realm. We begin to see ourselves devoted to our spouses. This happens because now trust is not just a word but a reality and whatever happens I cannot break or allow anything to come in the middle of my loyalty to the one God has given me for life. Our pledge to each other has to be built first on the foundation being faithful to God and the things that pleases Him. And faithfulness in a marriage does please God.

All through scripture God refers to adultery (the sexual unfaithfulness of a husband or a wife in thought and act) and the effects it has afterwards. He looks at unfaithfulness to Him as in a marriage:

Mark 7:19-21, Because it entereth not into his heart, but into the belly, and goeth out into the draught, purging all meats? 20 And he said, That which cometh out of the man, that defileth the man. ²¹ *For from within, out of the heart of men, proceed evil thoughts, adulteries, fornications, murders.*

Exodus 20:14, Thou shalt not commit adultery.

Proverbs 6:32, But whoso committeth adultery with a woman lacketh understanding: he that doeth it destroyeth his own soul.

Jeremiah 3:8-9, And I saw, when for all the causes whereby backsliding Israel committed adultery I had put her away, and given her a bill of divorce; yet her treacherous sister Judah feared not, but went and played the harlot also, ⁹ *And it came pass through the lightness of her whoredom, that she defileth the land, and committed adultery with stones and with stocks.*

Many of these travesties of broken faithfulness can be avoided if the marriage take on the Joshua mentality: *__And if it seem evil unto you to serve the LORD, choose you this day whom ye will serve; whether the gods which your fathers served that were on the other side of the flood, or the gods of the Amorites, in whose land ye dwell: but as for me and my house, we will serve the LORD (Joshua 24:15).__*

This was a pretty bold statement of faithfulness to God that Joshua made openly to the people. Because Joshua maintained this attitude all during his life as a Hebrew conqueror, it caused a "ripple effect" of blessings to overtake him and his family. We have to realize that only faithfulness to God will keep our marriages pure and dedicated so that when troubles rise and it will rise, then the two of you can stand as ONE and boldly declare that:

No weapon that is formed against thee shall prosper; and every tongue that shall rise against thee in judgment thou shalt condemn. This is the heritage of the servants of the LORD (the faithful of the Lord), and their righteousness is of me, saith the LORD (Isaiah 54:17).

☑ **Remember to always put God first in all you do, and He will not leave you but direct your marriage in the way of love and prosperity.**

A Marriage Prayer

Lord Jesus, we pray that you will lead and direct us in everything we do. We will from this moment on acknowledge you in all that we do and be led by your Holy Spirit. Take us into the path of righteousness for your name sake. Amen.

Chapter 3

Who Told You God Joined You Together?

Wherefore they are no more twain, but one flesh. What therefore God hath joined together, let not man put asunder (Matthew 19:6).

Many times, couples are brought together through different circumstances. There are diverse methods that have been introduced to society all through the beginning of time. Some of these have been through family gatherings, social clubs, single ministry, casual meetings, internet dating, blind dates and many other ways that have been shared. Some of the means are yet to be proven that it is a safe and effective way to meet the spouse of your choice. In all that there is, still the only way that tells you it is safe and will be blessed and that is the joining by God. How can you be sure that God truly did join you together? What are some of the signs you should detect that this man or woman was sent by God to be your life long mate? Let us explore some of the most ordained, romantic love relationships in the Bible.

First were our Patriarch and Matriarch of all patriarchs and matriarchs; "Adam and Eve". The book of Genesis or the book of "beginnings" describes a couple who was made for each other... so to speak. God already had in mind what He was going to do:

19

And God said, Let us make man in our image, after our likeness: and let them have dominion over the fish of the sea, and over the fowl of the air, and over the cattle, and over all the earth, and over every creeping thing that creepeth upon the earth. So God created man in his own image, in the image of God created he him; male and female created he them (Genesis 1: 27, 26).

We have to realize that in everything God does He has a plan and an order.

What are the things you began to look at when looking for that mate to spend the rest of your life with? Consider the pattern given by God. He first established a surrounding of safety and peace. God then created Adam and after that He gave instructions to Adam on how to care for it; then he introduced Eve into his life.

And the Lord God took the man and put him into the Garden of Eden to dress it and to keep it (Genesis 2:15).

The passage stated Adam had to "dress it." The Hebrew word for **dress** means to work, to serve. God was instructing Adam and giving him the mind of a developer. As a developer, he was to protect everything that was in his care. Protect from intruders; keep out anything that could cause damage, to put a hedge around. This is such an awesome statement and responsibility. So many times, marriages are attacked by different types of intruders that cause much damage. You have intruders of family, intruders of debt, intruders of lust, intruders of dishonesty, etc…

As the male, there should first be a hedge built up that would keep away the many obstacles that try to slip in unannounced and cause chaos.

Has the male mate begun to establish the surrounding of peace and security? You see God did not bring Eve on the scene just to let her feel goose bumps. God had everything that was necessary for Adam to provide for his new mate. Adam had to willingly assume the role of provider in order to make the union between he and his bride complete. God did not wait until He brought Eve on the scene to give Adam the provisions; when Eve arrived, Adam had what she needed to live as one. Too many times we come into marriage struggling and this curse seems to take over and ruin everything it can within the marriage. Struggle carries other symptoms called stress, depression, low self-esteem, confusion and strife. These are major symptoms that can inhabit our children and others that are closely around us. Because of these things many feel overwhelmed and start to give up, but I am here to tell you that many marriages have survived and been built strongly on having a lack of. And it is still because of the strength of the two to come together and press for what could be better that they succeed. On the other hand, more than too many marriages have resulted in divorce and separation because of the poverty-stricken nature they were married in and continued in. Yes, love is very important, but survival is a necessity.

EVE – THE HELP MEET

Let's talk about Eve. When she was introduced to her husband she was known to Adam as his counterpart.

And the Lord God said, it is not good that the man should be alone; I will make him an help meet for him (Genesis 2:18).

Let's look at the words *"help meet"*. The [3]Dake Bible describes these words as help suitable to man intellectually, morally, and physically. The word **help** signifies to give aid or assistance; to relieve; to further the advancement of; to change for the better; to refrain from. So many times, we fail to look for certain qualities in a person before we decide if this is the one for me.

- Is the female mate a person who has helped you to see she is always there to support you in what you are doing as long as it brings positive results within the family structure?
- Does she take joy in wanting to relieve you temporarily so that you can gain more strength and knowledge in your plans to succeed?
- Does she know how to refrain or back off when she sees you embarking into something new that can further develop your visions even if it means she don't always understand?

We must understand that to help sometimes means to leave alone. It's not always easy because most of the time woman like to know what is going on. That's when we must have patience and trust in the person we will call our spouse.

The woman must project to her husband a sense that "I have chosen this man for my mate and because of that I know:

- *Intellectually* he is the most resourceful, creative man I know;
- *Morally,* he has set in his heart to serve God and do whatever it takes to please Him first then his wife;
- *Physically,* he will always know that I will care for him in sickness and in health. Whether it is bodily or mentally."

A dedicated wife will always be there to encourage, give confidence, support and even to persuade her husband to go forward as she stands on the principals of Philippians *4:13, I can do all things through Christ which strengthens me.* Therefore, let's begin to ask ourselves the question again, "Who told me God joined us together?" One thing is for sure we need to know without any hesitation that God has formed this union and because of that it does not matter what obstacles or test are going to come our way because we know that "*4all things work together for good to them that love God, to them who are the called according to his purpose.*" Marriages ordained by God have a purpose and a plan; regardless of the purpose, it is for your good. God is not putting people together for good looks and personality; but you are being established and equipped to accomplish some major designs that He pre-destined for your marriage. Major dynasties and countries will be brought forth from your womb spiritually and naturally. Therefore, it is not wise to bond up with someone you are not equally yoked with. Being yoked together is going to cause you to feel the same hurt, feel the same disappointments, share the same joys, and excitements. These are but a few examples of the qualities we need to look for when coming together as one. Even during our time of marriage now for those of us whom the bond of matrimony has already been established, we need to consider changing our way of loving each other, examine ourselves and be honest when we ask ourselves, "Are we being what God has ordained for us to be to our spouses?

I know that, whatsoever God doeth, it shall be for ever: nothing can be put to it, nor anything taken from it: and God doeth it, that men should fear before him. (Ecclesiastes 3:14).

A Marriage Prayer

Dear Lord, As you joined Adam and Eve and told them they were as one, we ask that you make our union as one. Help us to know that you joined us together and no man can come between us. Amen.

Chapter 4

What is Intimacy?

My beloved spake, and said unto me, Rise up, my love, my fair one, and come away (Song of Solomon 2:10).

*W*ebster's dictionary describes *intimate* as such: *to announce formally; declare; to communicate indirectly; belonging to or characterizing one's deepest nature; marked by very close association or contact.*

I want us to look at intimacy as a form of strong communication. Intimacy is something that is developed over time between two people. It brings in a mutual level of trust and freedom to each party to express their inner most secrets and thoughts to each other, therefore giving each mate a since of awareness for the other's desires and inhibitions. Without communication, there can be no intimacy. Intimacy requires a person to take off the mask of pretense and be the real individual that God has created them to be. Because communication is highly observed it causes each other to begin to explore and learn what the vital points of interest and concerns for our mates. It reaches to the deepest level of the heart to learn more about the person that God is joining to their life. Communication brings out intimacies which causes a sensitivity of care, kindness, affection, and yes, love.

You cannot become totally intimate with your mate until you have established an open and honest line of

25

communication. Anything other than that is a forced relationship, which a lot of times are the basis of a marriage, whether good or bad.

Intimacy through communication can speak on what pleases one another and what concerns one another. For too long we have been building relationships on **LUST** and not **LOVE**!

"Communication inspires love and love
Welcomes intimacy."

At the heart of marriage is communication and intimacy, which both husband and wife must promote.

Genesis 2:21-25
21 And the Lord God caused a deep sleep to fall upon Adam, and he slept: and he took one of his ribs, and closed up the flesh instead thereof;

22 And the rib, which the Lord God had taken from man, made he a woman, and brought her unto the man.

23 And Adam said, This is now bone of my bones, and flesh of my flesh: she shall be called Woman, because she was taken from out of Man.

24 Therefore shall a man leave his father and his mother, and shall cleave unto his wife: and they shall be one flesh.

25 And they were both naked the man and his wife, and were not ashamed.

Adam begin to speak what he felt about his new bride, the one he was overwhelmed by and looked at as his cherished treasure. He assured her of his intentions. He communicated to her that she was now part of him to love. He did not look upon Eve as his maid servant or his concubine, but his wife. Adam was establishing the foundation for a long and prosperous marriage.

The bible says that because of Adam's words to his wife, the two of them were not ashamed of revealing themselves to each other. It describes them as being naked and not ashamed. They did not have to hide anything from each other as we do so many times in marriage.

If both spouses can't see what each other is doing, then eventually this can cut off the communication which can silence intimacy in your marriage. It can also allow for suspicion, envy, jealousy and strife to enter into the relationship. Learn how to first make your spouse your best friend with whom you can discuss those details with, but also be willing to listen to the other side as well.

☑ *Remember: It's Not Always About Sex!*
So then, we see intimacy does not always mean sex. Sexual desires are promoted through communication. You can become just as appealing to your spouse just by what you express to them, not what you have to get from them. God created sex and intimacy, and it is holy and good when enjoyed within the bounds of marriage. A husband and wife honor God when they love and enjoy each other.

AND, WHAT ABOUT SEX?

Marriage is honourable in all, and the bed undefiled (Hebrews 13:4).

Sex is God's gift to His creation. He endorses sex, and restricts it to those committed to each other in marriage. He wants sex to be motivated by love and commitment, not lust. It is for mutual pleasure, not selfish enjoyment. Both husbands and wives long for intimacy. But you must remember that men and women think differently when it comes to the way they want their desires fulfilled.

We need to learn to love to be loved. Sometimes it takes just holding hands to begin the romance. Our love for our spouse reveals them to be the most beautiful creatures in our sight. We should not look at them just for the physical attraction, but for the qualities that don't fade away such as, spiritual devotions, reliability, truthfulness, compassion, sensitivity and authenticity.

Yes, romance (candlelight dinners, walks in the park, date nights) can keep a marriage interesting, but commitment keeps romance alive. The trust that permeates the marriage is what allows the spouse to want their spouse to fulfill their inhibitions and desires.

I am my beloved's and my beloved is mine: he feedeth among the lilies (Song of Solomon 6:3).

A Marriage Prayer

Lord, we realize that without us knowing how to love You first then it is impossible to really love. Give us a passion and desire for each other and not a feeling of guilt and shame. Let us see the romance in each other's eyes and always have the zeal to be with each other always. Show us how to communicate positively and establish the trust that is needed to give us the joy we anticipate from each other. This we ask in the precious name of Jesus. Amen.

Chapter 5

Doing the Right Thing, Even if it Means Not Winning!

A wrathful man stirreth up strife: but he that is slow to anger appeaseth strife (Proverbs 15:18).

Surely the churning of milk bringeth forth butter, and the wringing of the nose bringeth forth blood: so the forcing of wrath bringeth forth strife (Proverbs 30:33).

Let us therefore follow after the things which make for peace, and things wherewith one may edify another (Romans 14:19).

And above all things have fervent charity among yourselves: for charity shall cover the multitude of sins (1 Peter 4:8).

So, what is right? In every relationship, there will be times when disagreement will happen. Through much prayer and wisdom, we can learn how to settle our differences. The majority of the time if we do not seek wise counsel and obey the Word of God, our unresponsiveness can cause very serious damage to marriage.

Discussion is always the best way to handle such crisis. If couples can't handle conversing with each other about what has caused a concern or variance between the two, it can create friction. This can be done without raising the

29

voice above the normal barriers of speech. Becoming aroused does not settle anything it just adds to the fire. Angered tempers, challenging words, spoken threats can be the ending results of this type of dispute.

I like Proverbs 30:33 when it says when you churn butter you will get milk and if you turn and twist on the nose it is truly going to bleed; so, the same if you agitate an angry person; you will get a fight. Therefore, it is better to lose the fight and win the battle. You don't always have to have your way, even if you are right. Learn sometimes to walk away from the dispute rather than beating a dead horse to prove your side. Learn to be silent in the middle of the heat and watch the fire dwindle down. It takes two to argue and one to think about the reason for the argument. Remember, a soft answer turns away wrath; BUT grievous words stir up anger (Proverbs 15:1).

BUT, in walking away never leave with the intention of making your spouse feel belittled or defenseless. Always try to:

1. **Make an effort to calm the situation.**
2. **Make a point of letting them know that you understand the importance of their concern and the two of you will come to an understanding.**
3. **Work out the misunderstanding so that the problem will not arise again.**

Keep in mind it's not a matter of who's right or wrong but what the two of you can learn to live with. What's right is always a matter of what that person might have been brought up in.

Example:
Husbands might think it's okay to leave the toilet seat

up if they were never taught as a young lad to put it down after using it. So, in their mindset, "What's the harm in the wife putting it down if she needs to use it." This of course, can really agitate wives because who wants to pull down something they never put out of position anyway. Consequently, the compromise can be just pull the whole tank cover down as a practice; this allows for the beauty of the toilet to be displayed and gives less opportunity for anything to fall in it (smile).

IS IT A LITTLE TOO DARK RIGHT NOW?

Be ye angry, and sin not: let not the sun go down upon your wrath: (Ephesians 4:26).

Conflict can make you tired and disgusted. So, it is always better to try to call a truce when weariness begins to come. Always try to settle your difference of opinions before saying goodnight or goodbye for the day. After all you never know when you will see your lover again and you don't want to end your evening on a sour note.

- But what if the fight was intense and heated and hurtful things were said?
- *What* if I don't feel like forgiving my spouse?
- What then?

Well, the Word of God is clear and plain on the topic of forgiveness.

Colossians 3:13, Forbearing one another, and forgiving one another, if any man have a quarrel against any: even as Christ forgave you, so also do ye.

Matthew 11:25, And when ye stand praying, forgive, if ye have ought against any: that your Father also which is in heaven may forgive you your trespasses.

31

Yes, the words hurled at you hurt, the accusations left a mark on your heart, but before you lay your head down for sleep, you must forgive, even if the matter you disagreed about is not settled.

Make sure your spouse knows that they are loved. Just as absence makes the heart grow fonder, it can also make the heart feel angry. How you leave your spouse can affect your whole day and night. Departing in anger can cause you to be upset with everyone around you and be in doubt of other people's attempts to do right. It can cause you to become vulnerable. You will be tempted to make decisions based on what you feel for the moment and not what is absolutely right for the rest of your life.

Bring to a halt and smolder out the fire of anger. This can keep out all types of feelings of anguish that will eventually come back to haunt your nuptials.

Things to Remember:

1. Don't let a mole hill build over time into a volcanic explosion. If something is bothering you, then tell your spouse.
2. If you are angry about something wait for the right time to speak with your spouse about it, but don't wait too long.
3. If your spouse shows no interest in the topic you wish to discuss, then make an appointment with them.
4. What happens in your marriage, stays in your marriage, unless otherwise agreed upon to share with your pastor/counselor. Third parties, such as in-laws, best friends or your children is forbidden.

5. When having a disagreement, no hitting below the belt by drudging up past history. Respect your spouse.
6. Fighting fair means no name calling. Even endearing terms and pet names can be hurtful when you are using a sarcastic tone.
7. Listen to one another fully while you fight. This includes watching body language. Make eye contact when you speak.
8. Don't interrupt with your thoughts while your spouse is speaking. .
9. Fighting fair means you don't blame one another or make accusations.
10. We tend to make our spouse the bad guy when describing our feelings, so try to use 'I' sentences instead of 'you' sentences.
11. If the two of you are not extremely angry, try to hold hands while talking during your fight.
12. Always be open to asking for forgiveness and being willing to forgive.

FIGHT FAIR

It's a given that as a married couple there will be differences or fights. How you fight is the key to whether or not you will have a successful, long-term marriage. Fighting fairly with respect for one another is a critical marital skill that you must learn.

- **Tips:**

    ➢ No name calling – Ephesians 4:26 -32
    ➢ Respect one another – Ephesians 5:21-33
    ➢ Don't be petty – Philippians 2:3-5

> ➢ Don't be childish – 1 Corinthians 13:4-8
> ➢ Dwell in unity – Psalm 133
> ➢

IT'S NOT ABOUT YOU!

Rejoice with them that do rejoice, and weep with them that weep (Romans 12:15).

What concerns your spouse should concern you. If it is important enough to your spouse to cause them to be upset it should be just as important to you. Never tell your spouse that *"it does not matter",* because it does! Your interest of their crisis should always be of love and reassurance. What disturbs their peace will ultimately disrupt your peace if not handled properly. You won't see the solution if you are always looking at the problem. Don't try and change the person but try and find a solution to the problem.

A Marriage Prayer

Lord we need you to teach us how to be agreeable in our disagreement. Teach us how to grow in your character with your fruit of the Spirit in us to discourage any anger, malice or wicked feelings, thoughts and actions that we might have displayed towards our spouse in the past.

Lord we ask that You help us to remember that as a married person, we are no longer to think of only what is important to ourselves. But what is best for our marriage. Amen.

Chapter 6

Handle Your Business

Luke 14:28-30, For which of you, intending to build a tower, sitteth not down first, and counteth the cost, whether he have sufficient to finish it?

[29] Lest haply, after he hath laid the foundation, and is not able to finish it, all that behold it begin to mock him,

[30] Saying, This man began to build, and was not able to finish.

In the present day, it is a well-known fact that the lack of money has been the cause of division in most families. All through history stories have been told one by one about children growing up without both parents because one left, more often than not the male, to seek a better life. This often was searched out through a better job to obtain more money and in the end it basically split up the family and put more hardship on the one parent that generally stayed forcing them to work many hours for little wages.

Today with this generation seeking more careers and entrepreneurship you would think that money would not be an issue. Surprise, it's even worse. The more money most people make the more they need. The more they need the more they strive to get, by any means possible. Husbands and wives are working overtime, time and a half, double time, Sunday's time and whatever type of time

35

they can get to put more on their paycheck. The true essence of this reality is that God says that if you seek the kingdom of God, and his righteousness; and all these things shall be added unto you (**Matthew 6:33**). We have to understand that if God says He is the provider of all our needs, however He provides it, means that He is giving us just what we need to live abundantly. The question we have to ask is, "Are we good stewards over what God gives us?"

WHAT IS A STEWARD?

Luke 12:42, And the Lord said, Who then is that faithful and wise steward, whom his lord shall make ruler over his household, to give them their portion of meat in due season?

Now, let's look in detail at the expectations God has for a potential steward.

1. *House Agent* – One that acts on behalf of their household.

2. *Manager* – one that can control and make wise decisions that will affect the welfare of those under their domain; can assign tasks to reliable people without being critical and overbearing.

3. *Servant* – one who does not mind humbling themselves to serve when necessary to make things work out.

4. *Responsible* - willing and able to fulfill one's obligations; able to choose between right and wrong; liable to be called upon to give satisfaction (as for losses and misdeeds).

5. _**Trainer of the heir**_ – to be able to teach by example, instruction and patience.

I truly believe that when we do right over the little things God will make us rulers over many things, without us being too worn out to enjoy them.

Because of the impact that the lack of money has on our households it is imperative that whatever you are filtering in now in the area of money you must try to budget. Both spouses should be involved in this area so that one would always know what the other is doing and how it is being done. As a rule of thumb whoever is the stronger at something usually can handle that part of the marriage. But with money because it carries so many stigmas and can cause both pain and joy, the knowledge of it needs to be shared by both parties. In other words, at least once a month both husband and wife need to sit down and discuss what was taken in and what was spent out thereby reconciling their books for the month on one accord. It's a hard thing when one is spending money and the other doesn't know where the money is, or thinks there is more than it is. This should be whether both parties are working or not. The more you know together the less possibility there is of confusion and strife coming into the relationship. Two is always better than one.

This method can alleviate any mistrust as to the finances. Sometimes this can also allow you to see where the finances is coming up short and what solutions can be used to remedy the situation. Many times, a spouse establishes a weekly allowance (believe me, this is not a bad thing) so that each one can learn how to gain self-control over their spending habits. _**1 Tim 6:10 says, for the**_ *love of money is the root of all evil:* so, when you find yourself not being able to control your spending then you know you are putting money over everything else in your life.

Solomon advised that money if handled properly *"can answer all things"* (**Ecclesiastes 10:19**).

☑ **Remember this:**

- Know your limitations and follow them.
- Plan for your future because it really does not belong to you but to the one you expect to benefit from your inheritance. A wise man leaves a nest of wealth to those he has been an example to.
- Don't determine your wealth on how much you have, but build it on how you obtained it. It's not how much money you have but what you are doing with what's been placed in your care.

LONG TERM BENEFITS

Another thing you want to remember is when it's your time to leave this world don't leave your worries in the world. Your worries quickly turn into someone else's burden. Plan ahead for your family as to what they will need when you are not around. Sacrifice now, to make sure that you are insured with enough for your spouse to bury you and plan to live comfortably without any stress for at least one year; giving them time to learn how to invest and make the money you have left work for them. Making payments on things such as cars, homes, credit cards, utilities and etc. are still going to continue. Many families lose a great deal of possessions after one of the spouses die because of mismanagement of money. **Cover Yourself**

38

Adequately!!! Start out gradually with what you can afford and slowly increase the value as you get increase. These are things that you know you will need to make sure your part of being a good steward is in motion.

Make sure important documents that carry any value on them are accessible during a time of distress and despair so that frustration and panic won't come into making any decisions. Make sure you have a will. The will is a conveyance paper expressing your desire to assure that your spouse has complete control to make any choices they need without the procedure of any courts and lawyers which can take away from your inheritance you left for your family. This is especially recommended for couples who have been married more than once and have other children from previous marriages or relationships.

☑ **Remember to:**

- Seize the time to handle your finances and seek the guidance of God in everything you do. (If you plan ahead you stand less of a chance of being surprised.)
- Never borrow money to pay off a debt, but borrow to invest.
- Your finances are your business and not your neighbors or your family so keep them out of it.

Whether you have enough or not enough money, learn to work your finances together. If you feel that a financial advisor is necessary, then seek the credentials of one and by all means try to let it be a God-fearing advisor.

A Marriage Prayer

Lord we realize that in order to grow in You both spiritually and naturally we have to become good stewards over what You have given us. First let us come into agreement that we are to bring to you the first fruit of all our increase and then You will teach us how to produce the harvest You have planned for us.

Chapter 7

How Can Two Walk Together If They Don't Agree?

Amos 3:3 Can two walk together, except they be agreed?

What is the definition of "agree"? How do most people look at the term agreement? These are questions that we have to ask ourselves sometimes. If we just answered out of our heads most of us would say to agree means to think on the same terms. Too come to some sort of mutual understanding. But let's look at this a little closer.

[6]Webster's school dictionary describes agree as; 1) **having consent**, 2) **to give one's approval**, 3) **to concede**. *WOW*! Look at these meanings with respect to your relationship. This complete implication is that I can no longer think about myself but I must consider the position of someone else even if it means that my way of doing things must pass on.

First, let's study the concept of *"having consent"*. Consenting is giving authorization. In our relationships, this means we have to give permission to the other's needs more often than our own. We have to stop looking at the big "**I**" and focus on the "**US**". Sometimes it causes our way of thinking to be put on hold if it means the safety and welfare of our mates. Don't always spend your every

41

moment on your dreams and visions; find out what are your spouse's concerns, thoughts and desires. See what you can do to be a part of what is in their heart, but make sure it is for the advancement of you both. Remember, your dreams might be different but in the end, they will correspond. They will enhance each other.

Philippians 2:2, Fulfil ye my joy, that ye be likeminded, having the same love, being of one accord, of one mind.

3 Let nothing be done through strife or vainglory; but in lowliness of mind let each esteem the other better than themselves.

Two people can preach the same gospel but do it differently and bring in the same results. What's more important? Bringing in the result or doing it your way?

Allow yourself to come into a position of willingness to *"give your approval"* for the things that are suggested to make your connection even healthier. Learn to say "yes" sometimes even if it's against your "norm." Change is good even if you might not understand it and the idea did not come from you. God does not give all the brains to one person in the relationship. Stop saying "no" and learn to listen and try new ideas. New concepts always work best when they are tried in agreement.

This brings us to concede sometimes. It's not about you all the time! (*Remember Chapter 5, Doing the Right Thing, Even If It Means Not Winning!*) Yes, learn this secret revelation and it can take you a long way in your relationship. You don't have to have your way all the time. There is nothing worse than a spoiled child who feels that they can punish their parent by always trying to get their way through embarrassing moments, ignoring them, sulking or even targeting them for despair. As you begin to grow in your relationship you should always be concerned with your attitude. Stop expecting to always get your way and learn to concede. I have news for you, the world does not stop rotating if you don't get your way; you just make it harder for you to find peace in all that you do. Sometimes getting your way can be very detrimental to your cause.

Always try the three concepts of **consent, approval &
concede**. This will walk you into a much more balanced marriage.

Ephesians 4:29-32,
[29] *Let no corrupt communication proceed out of your mouth,
but that which is good to the use of <u>edifying</u>, that it may
<u>minister</u> grace unto the hearers.*

[30] *And grieve not the Holy Spirit of God, whereby ye are
sealed unto the day of redemption.*

[31] *Let all bitterness, and wrath, and anger, and clamour
(insistent protest or demand), and evil speaking, be put away
from you, with all malice:*

[32] *And be ye kind one to another, tenderhearted, forgiving one
another, even as God for Christ's sake hath forgiven you.*

Paul instructs to build up (edify) and to serve (minister) the other rather than always wanting your way. This is the same that Christ did for us. Let's love more and give more rather than always trying to take, take, and take.

A Marriage Prayer

Lord, teach me to be more agreeable in those things that will help my marriage become stronger and more loving. Let me not think only on myself but see my spouse as the person that you have divinely joined me to therefore realizing that we can come to an understanding and walk together in love.

Chapter 8

Partners for Life

"I take thee to be my wedded spouse, to have and to hold, from this day forward, for better for worse, for richer, for poorer, in sickness and in health, to love and to cherish, <u>till death us do part</u>, <u>according to God's holy ordinance</u>; and thereto I plight thee my troth (loyal or pledged faithfulness)."

Partners for life begins when you come to the understanding of who God has given you to be with in a lifetime of togetherness. Lifetimes of emotions, challenges, possibilities, love, etc. Whom God has joined together let no man put asunder (tear you apart). Through the good times and the rough, God is still in your union. Whether you are rich in spirit or prosperous in love, this marriage is yours for keeps. Don't even think of divorce as an option for solving conflicts of disagreements. Learn how to love each other for the differences you make to each other.

☑ **REMEMBER,** there is a difference between disagreements and abuse. Physical abuse is never a marriage it is a single party rule. Mental abuse is dictatorship. If you find yourself in any one of these types of relationship, **please seek help** **immediately**.

- Physical abuse is anyone of the parties either male or female who feel that they have the right to strike their mate for any reason.

45

- Verbal abuse is when one of the mates speak harshly or insensitively to the other therefore making them feel that they are inferior and have no opinion whatsoever in the building of their relationship.

Both are generally done through someone who is insecure and rebels back at the weaker character in the marriage.

Uncover the strength within you. Then with the help of His Holy Spirit, go to your Pastor and request help. Many times, these types of relationships end up deadly. This is not expressing love to you.

1 Corinthians 13:4, Charity (love) suffereth long, and is kind; charity envieth not; charity vaunteth not itself, is not puffed up,

5 Doth not behave itself unseemly, seeketh not her own, is not easily provoked, thinketh no evil;

Life is choice driven and you can choose to take your relationship to greater qualities of living. Don't ever give up on your mate or yourself. Stop trying to change your mate and work on changing you. Your marriage is an awesome weapon against the enemy, because he comes to cause division and strife. Once you stop allowing Satan to come infiltrate your bond you can win every battle you come up against together.

Remember,
How should one chase a thousand, and two put ten thousand to flight, except their Rock had sold them, and the LORD had shut them up (Deuteronomy 32:30)?

There is power in unity. Unity grows through endurance. Two can stand stronger than one.

And if one prevail against him, two shall withstand him; and a threefold cord is not quickly broken (Ecclesiastes 4:12).

With you, your spouse and His Holy Spirit you shall prevail! Know that God did not call you to quit the race, but to keep going until the race has been won.

A Marriage Prayer

Lord I truly pray that You keep the significance of nuptials within our hearts and teach us that You have coupled us together to be one and not two. Let us see each other as we've never seen each other before. As we mature together that we will cultivate more love for each other as the day we met. Help us to not see the other's faults but see ourselves so that we can began to choose what is good for us. I thank You God for this lifetime membership that You have placed in my care. I promise to love, honor and respect all that this union is to me. In Lord Jesus' name, I pray. Amen.

About the Author

S.J. Boykin resides in Hollywood, Florida with her husband Apostle Benjamin J. Boykin. She serves as Chaplain and Pastor. Chaplain Boykin along with her husband have come together on many occasions to minister to couples both married, engaged and single. Together they pastor True Fellowship Worship Center in Hollywood, Florida. Chaplain Boykin is also the founder of True Fellowship Chaplain Academy of South Florida.

God has taken what they call a family of diversity and used it for ministry. They are the parents of 6 children and many grandchildren. They also enjoy the host of spiritual sons and daughters that God has given them along with special friends of the Gospel.

Chaplain Boykin's desire is that families all over the nations come together as one regardless of ethnicity and cultural differences. A strong family whose faith is in God can become serious kingdom builders. We need to begin to encourage, instruct and pray for the family values that God has given us from the beginning.

For speaking engagements, seminars or books please contact Chaplain Boykin:

True Fellowship Worship Center Office
P.O. Box 813299
Hollywood, Florida 33021-3299

Website: sjb.hischaplains.com
Email: sjb@hischaplains.com

Endnotes

Chapter 1
[1] "Marriage," Merriam Webster's student dictionary. Retrieved from http://www.merriam-webster.com/dictionary/marriage

Chapter 2
[2] "Faithful," Merriam Webster's student dictionary. Retrieved from http://www.merriam-webster.com/dictionary/faithful

Chapter 3
[3] The Dake Annotated Bible, Dake Publishing, 2015
[4] Romans 8:28, Holman Bible Publishers, 1996

Chapter 4
[5] "Intimate," Merriam Webster's student dictionary. Retrieved from http://www.merriam-webster.com/dictionary/intimate

Chapter 7
[6] "Agree," Merriam Webster's student dictionary. Retrieved from http://www.merriam-webster.com/dictionary/agree